Table of Contents

As a free show of my appreciation to my readers, I've put together 10 Lessons For Turning An Employee Into An Entrepreneur.

To get the free eBook go to the website and sign up. It will be automatically delivered to your email.

Going beyond the boundaries of coaching

What if your people led regardless the role they hold in your organization?

What if your people wanted to take part in change initiatives?

What if professional development left your people with a practical route forward?

Leadership coaching is the essential tool for changing an organization. As you know, change is fundamental for organizations to grow and adjust to today's transient shifting marketplace, yet people and organizations are immune to change.

Leadership coaching can hasten efficacious changes in teams, employees, and systems by clarifying visions, beliefs, values, strengthening knowledge and enabling leaders, managers and employees to uncover their full potential.

Coaching people can help them to eliminate the consequences of negative emotions such as fear–the most inhibitive feelings, guilt and worry. Fear is the most important emotion that you have to change because it can influence your personal life and your career, keeping you away from challenges and accomplishments.

To coach people you firstly need to be an efficient leader with vision, determination, integrity, motivation in order to improve and encourage people, strong and effective communication skills and positive thinking and what is the most important-empathy.

Nowadays, coaching has become a booming niche of development because the business environment is a competitive arena where everyone is struggling for their purposes and dreams, jobs are more complex than in the past, the challenges are more complicated, rapid changes arise every moment, organizations have to understand and solve people's issues and needs.

"Each person holds so much power within themselves that needs to be let out. Sometimes they just need a little nudge, a little direction, a little support, a little coaching, and the greatest things can happen."

Coaching has become the art of leading people to outstanding results and achievements because it goes beyond mentoring and therapy and teaches you how to implement the successful idea for a successful life.

As the environment around us changes every day, coaching is needed more than ever before to solve the problem of the offset between the new mentality and prerequisite skills and the old mentality.

The world is changing with the speed of light, information and breakthrough keep succeeding with an incommensurable pace. If you want to keep up, you have to advance continually, to face challenges and to follow courses and training where necessary.

Flexibility is the key tool of personal and professional success in this chaotic life. We have to adjust our mind rapidly to new era expectations and to be very flexible with all the things are happening around us. We have to be committed and learn every day other things.

This epoch is not only asking for speed and creativity but also for entrepreneurship attitude.

Can be leadership taught?

The ability to lead is not a trait that you are automatically born with, like blond hair or blue eyes. You may have an opportunity to lead, but you will not immediately knowhow, like some gift granted to you at birth. You have to learn how to be a leader, and it is not easy. You have to want it, and then put the effort into developing those leadership skills.

I learned about leadership from the best boss that I ever had. He taught me that leaders start with clear goals, clearly communicate their vision, and then lead from the front. That's leadership and it can be learned through earnest self-awareness and hard work.

I have never forgotten those lessons:

Develop your strategy

You must first have a plan that people can get behind. Pinpoint one problem, and then delineate your vision for solving it. Establish a set of goals that you want to achieve and then communicate this strategy to the people you hope to lead. As you knock out those goals, set new ones that align to your strategy. In this way, you will start to build momentum.

Get out in front

You cannot be a leader by just sitting back and passively observing others as they tackle all the work. You need them more than they need you, so start acting like it. Prove yourself worthy of leading by working as hard — or even harder — than everyone else. When others see that you have a real stake in the success or failure of the project, you will begin to earn their loyalty.

Keep moving

You will make many mistakes as a leader, and some will be bigger than others. Do not give up at the first failure or remain blind to the reasons you stumbled. Instead, allow your failures to teach you how to be a better leader. Be honest with yourself and transparent with others. Evaluate, adjust and move on.

Remain humble

Once you start hitting your goals, you will begin to feel more comfortable as a leader. But as your confidence and authority grows, so can your ego. Do not let that happen. Remember the people who have helped you get where you are. You are standing on their shoulders. Always be mindful of the people on your team and throw credit their way. Admit to your shortcomings and lead with humility.

Continue learning

Make it a point to further your knowledge, especially when you think you have learned everything there is to know. When it comes to learning about leadership, I have found that there is no "done!" Every day will present new situations and challenges, and if you remain open to the learning opportunity, you will never be bored.

Inspire and motivate

No matter how good you are, you will only be as successful as your team. So … getting the most from each team member is critical. We call this being a multiplier leader. Multiplier leaders know the importance of bringing out the smarts and capabilities in everyone around them.

Balancing listening

Part of the balancing is going beyond hearing to develop your full sense of listening. This includes watching body language and observing emotions. If you don't listen in this way you'll miss plenty of opportunities to learn and connect to others. Great leaders understand the impact of words that can hurt, anger, or create fear. They know that when they say too much, others stop speaking and creativity and inclusion are a lost cause.

Foster teamwork

Peter Drucker made an interesting point when he said that leaders don't train themselves not to say "I." He's implying that leaders innately work with others and let the team get the credit. They don't force themselves to say "we." "We" is natural for them, and it's the way they've always thought.

It can be negative for an organization to have an "employee of the month" or a "who gets credit for what" attitude. You work as a team when you don't care who gets the credit. So the next time you see someone with a resume that states, "I accomplished x" or "I did x," it should send up a few warning signals.

Collaboration

It's important to know it is good to ask for help, advice and constructive criticism. There are very few places where a lone wolf leader can be effective. Decisions are complex, and it takes a village of smart people to help make them. Leaders who aren't inclusive may find that their organizations lack creativity.

No fear of daring choices

There's never one formula to achieve something. Don't be afraid to take a leap; even if the outcome is not ideal, it provides you with the opportunity to learn the next time around. Step out of rigid mindsets and explore new ideas outside your comfort zone.

Boost Team Self-Esteem

Employee attitude is so critical that it can't be overemphasized. It trickles down from employers. Your business can never be what it can be if you don't focus on employee happiness.

No matter, you'll have dozens of people criticize you. Customers, current and former employees, family, and friends may give you constructive criticism. It can be stressful to hear or read, and it can be easy to pass on criticism to employees. But it doesn't help. As a leader, you should ensure employees have high self-esteem in their job.

Leaders should make employees feel good about themselves. Constantly criticizing and pointing out the flaws in an employee is a sure fire way to decrease morale and performance.

Maintain work- life balance

While completing certain tasks and achieving success is the ultimate goal, it's important to have a work life balance so you don't burn yourself out. Lots of leaders espouse this balance, but only a rare few actually walk the talk. Great leaders can't say this and then work 60 or more hours per week.

Lead with questions, not directions

Rarely tell staff what to do. While that may seem the easiest way, it's more beneficial to help by allowing them to figure things out for themselves. The real learning is created within the team by ensuring that we're asking the right questions.

Patience

Many leaders are intolerant of others who might do things differently or at a pace the leader finds unacceptable. Action oriented leaders may have a tendency to jump to conclusions before things are thought through. The lack of patience can manifest itself as anger or decisions that aren't fully thought through. Be patient and reflective and always set aside thinking time. It is imperative for success.

Chapter 1: Learning the foundations of leadership

Leadership is often taken for granted but in fact it is not as simple as most people think. That is why some people excel in leadership while others fail. The presence of many leadership theories is a testament that it is a subject that has presented a challenge and thus elicited the contribution of different scholastic schools of thought. All these theories seem to endeavor to demystify leadership and make it understandable to many.

As such, this piece explores the Four

Core Theory Groups approach in leadership. To begin with, the Trait Theory is among the four group theories. This theory ordains that people succeed in leading while others fail because of their different personalities. Many of the early trait theories held that leadership is innate and that people could do nothing to be good leadership unless they were with the intrinsic abilities of a leader.

However, contemporary trait theories show that leadership is an art that can be perfected. Behavioral Theories are also part of the four core theory group. This kind of leadership study looks into how leaders behave or how they should behave. For instance, should leaders dictate what should be done and expect the unanimous cooperation of members or should they involve them in the decision-making process and then chart out the way forward together? Under this category, there are three cadres of leaders.

First, there are autocratic leaders who are despots who lead dictatorially. Again, there are democratic leaders who encourage team work and equal participation. Laissez-faire leaders also fall in this class and this is kind of leadership whereby subordinates are given the leeway to think on their won and execute their responsibilities as they deem fit.

Another among the four core theory group is the contingency theory that ordains that leaders behave the way they do because of the prevailing circumstances or situations. However, it has met a lot of acrid opposition from other schools of thought since it was widely believed that it is during a crisis that the true quality and character of leadership is tried and fire-furnaced.

The last of these theories is the Power and Influence Theories approach. This view of leadership analysis stipulates that a leader acts depending on the amount of power, mandate, or ambit under their jurisdiction.

For instance, how much power a leader has is thought to profoundly affect how they push their subordinates to get things done?

Chapter 2: Empathy–the tool for building people into groups

Empathy is an often misunderstood term. It is perhaps the most advanced skill in communication. Empathy is defined as the ability to see the world through another person's eyes, in other words, putting oneself in the shoes of others. It involves understanding another person's feelings, emotional state, and concerns.

Empathy is a selfless act that helps us

understand other people and create fraternal bonds with them. As such, people who are empathetic towards others are not just friends but soul mates. Having understood what empathy is, how can it help people form workable professional groups within an organization?

To begin with, people must not be groups simply because the supervisors have told them to coalesce into such units. For true work group to work, leader must understand his subordinates and empathy can help him attain this. Once the leader understands those under him, he is in a better position to help them.

Although empathy is an advanced communication weapon that many people lack, it is relieving to know that people must not be necessarily born with it since it can be cultivated or developed in people. As such, it is the onus of a great leader to create empathy among his subordinates and lead by example. It is his business to nurture empathy and steer feasible group work within the organization.

Again, a leader who lacks empathy would treat the divergent opinions of others as arrant nonsense. On the other hand, a leader who is empathetic towards others would not brush off their ideas. Instead, he would try to understand why other people choose to think the way they do. Once you understand the underlying principles or experiences that motivate another person's viewpoint, you are able to concur with them. However funny or bizarre others' ideas may sound, they have something that can help you shape your own vision. Even better, various opinions/ideas on the same subject should merge to form a superior opinion/amicable way forward. And since a leader should be the most tolerant member of the team, he must acquire and practice empathy.

Finally, any leader who cares about the organization must know that empathy creates a true sense of friendship and mutual respect within a group. Any group that lacks these two can only be a waste of time. Friendly people who respect each another tend to take each other's ideas positively and they try to learn at least something from them. When people within a group are ready to receive divergent opinions positively and broad-mindedly, group members can only have the sky as their limit.

Chapter 3: Authenticity -a key to brand success

It is disheartening to see the world so full of mimicry. People have given their originality to the dogs and have chosen to be copycats. You are the best person the world has ever known and you should love your original ideas. As such, it is more than suicidal to embrace other's ideas and write off your original own. True leaders value authenticity and originality because they know that these are the engines to building a powerful brand name. As such, this piece explores the importance of authenticity when promoting a brand. Three aspects of authenticity will be expounded. Read on to discover more.

Authenticity is Self-Definition

The worst thing about copying others and shunning being your original self is that you lose yourself definition. It is even ironical to copy others yet you want to be the champion in the industry. If you are doing what your rivals in the trade, then how will you attain the difference that should help you cut a niche of excellence and be a cut above the rest? It is heavily satirical to run a race at the pace of other runners and hope to cross the end line ahead of them. It is tantamount to eating one's cake and then hope to still have it.

Therefore, true leaders should go for authentic and original ideas that make them stand out of the clutter. Any you won't stand out of it unless you acquire yourself some measure of uniqueness. You should, however, note that the decision to chase uniqueness is a double-edged sword. You may chase uniqueness and self-definition for own sake until you lose sight of what you exactly like to achieve with your uniqueness.

Authenticity and Transparency Are Inseparable

A leader who embraces authenticity while promoting their brand also attains a good measure of transparency. Note that copycats cannot be fully transparent. Whether it is to one's subordinates or the outside public, authenticity cultivates a general sense of transparency. Transparency in turn inspires respect and confidence of those around you.

Therefore, you should always strive to be original and authentic as a leader. Note that choosing to follow the path of authenticity is not easy. It is the bold step that you must be willing to take. Contrariwise, mimicry is a luring path that may look promising but it is a short road that ends quickly. You must shun its easy lures and pay the cost of dreaming boldly authentic.

Chapter 4: Leadership as a blending of strategy and character

Blending character and strategy is the best approach to leadership. Strategy helps a leader know the prevailing situation and how to best work toward bettering the status quo. Both strategy and character are equally important in leadership. Since neither of them should be given higher priority because they are all important, they ought to be mixed in a balanced way. Therefore, this piece explores the reasons why any chartered and accomplished leader/coach must have both.

Even with the best strategy, a leader cannot discharge his responsibilities without a formidable character and personality. In many organizations, you will find very bright and able leaders who cannot lead simply because they have given their reputation/character to the dogs. Employees who do not hold their boss in high esteem, for example, cannot take them seriously even when their ideas are for everyone's good. That is why a leader must have both good strategy and a personality that is beyond reproach.

Strategy is born of a superior brain and character is born out of the richness of one's soul. In this case, a seasoned leader needs both a good personality and a strong character. This helps him convince those under them about what should be done in every situation. His experience/wisdom/knowledge comes in handy in designing the strategy. This way, he is able to win the support of those under him. However, for him to have the support of their subordinates, he ought to have won his confidence as well. It is however not possible to win the confidence of your subordinates unless they know that you are a person of a good-natured and well-meaning personality.

It is said that a superior brain may take you to the heavens, but it takes a sound character to stay there. A good leader who charts wonderful strategies that can take an organization to the clouds should also have the requisite character to maintain it there. In some situations, especially in a crisis, very stringent measures that require a lot of discipline to execute are needed. In this regard, the strategies are of little use without the availability of the required personality on the part of the leader/coach.

In conclusion, it is impossible to succeed as a leader/coach without a perfect balance between character and strategy. The first one is the engine that moves the locomotive of leadership while the latter is the wheel. Neither can be of any use without the perfect balance of the two.

Chapter 5: Fundamental traits for being a leader

A leader is a person given mandate to head, direct or represent others in a given field. Leadership is such an important role that has power and responsibility bestowed upon him or her. A leader must present and conduct himself to the public in a way that will build good rapport and relations to the audience.

A leader should, therefore, possess certain traits and characteristics that are the key in discharging the duties of service to others. These behavioral characteristics not only help the leader but also make those he leads to having confidence in him. These qualities are illustrated below.

Adjustment

It is the ability to change or to improve in order to adapt to the constantly changing environment. A leader should, therefore, be flexible enough to a state that best suits and is favorable to the willing majority. He or she must act in a way that is considered correct by the members of the group. It is mainly applied in problem-solving and coordinating the efforts of the members to work together.

Charisma

It is the capability of influencing a large group being able to introduce new ideas and ways of doing things. The leader is able to achieve this without creating ill feelings among the people. Such behavior is the manner in which the leader conducts himself or herself. It must be in a manner that is decent and socially acceptable.

Extraversion

It is a rare trait that any leader who is

focused towards excellence is required to embrace. It is the power of being happy in company of others as opposed to being alone. A leader cannot coordinate others of he or she is not able to associate with them by being social, assertive and talkative to understand their deep feelings and opinions of the organization.

Intelligence

Intelligence also comes handy when leaders are mentioned at any forum. As a leader, you should have the ability to acquire and apply knowledge and skills. You should be able to acquire the latest technics that are key in service delivery and in line with the visions and goals of the organization. It also demands a high capacity of the leader to learn and relate to the daily life experiences.

As discussed above the golden rules of leadership include charisma, extraversion, intelligence, adjustment, and behavior. These traits when combined with many others in a leader he or she will be a leader for people.

Chapter 6: Essence of Self-motivation in leadership coaching

Self-motivation is the force that drives and aids you to do things by yourself without being supervised, monitored, or forced to do them. It is the inner feeling that keeps one encouraged and going. While working towards achievement of the set goals, missions, and visions self-motivation is a very crucial virtue that any leader should have in order to effectively serve the people they are in charge of and achieve the goals they intend during their tenure.

First, self-motivation helps a leader develop a sense of positive attitude and development. A self-motivated leader shall always develop a good attitude and perception towards his responsibilities mandated to discharge. A positive attitude enhances effectiveness and hard work in a leader.

Secondly, self-motivation paves the way for the leader to be self-empowered and self-developed. This is a situation where a leader improves the quality of their leadership through experience while discharging the duties. Leadership is a career that entails much issues and roles. The leader usually deals with numerous problems as they carry out their duties. Through interaction with new people and situations, they understand ways of doing things a leader gains new knowledge and ideas on how to deal with various issues such as proper and effective evaluation and implementation of ideas and judgment. Consequently, a leader develops their self-worth.

Moreover, self-motivation helps a leader increase and improve the morale working of the junior employees who work under their supervision. The employees work to their utmost if the leader works as an example and role model for them. The junior employees shall only be encouraged to work harder and smarter if the leadership also performs and discharges its duties as required. As a result, teamwork, solidarity, and unity are enhanced. This in return creates an opportunity for the success of not only the employees but also the leader and the organization as a whole.

The art of personal organization in leadership also comes as a result of self-motivation. A self-motivated leader shall be able to finish the task assigned to do and attend to the roles in time.

Leadership entails the setting, achievement, and fulfillment of the goals by either the leader or the organization they are is in charge of. Realistic goals shall only be set and accomplished if the leader is self-motivated.

It is said that inner drive and desire that shall keep the leader are moving towards accomplishing the set goals, objectives and missions of an organization.

Chapter 7: Why should you be an authentic leader?

It is wise to keep a notch higher by realizing the pros and cons of being authentic as a leader. Becoming an authentic leader will require little effort but, more practice and enough patience. Here are qualities common to famous authentic leaders.

Being unique is what will attract the attention of multitudes and make their thinking fit with your own objectives. Furthermore, the similar the objectives the clearer the goals and faster the period spent convincing fellows who have different views towards life to work together.

Authenticity makes a leader be strictly objective minded. Being objective-minded is crucial because it brings you to a position of mobilizing dozens of individuals to a common goal, go ahead and state your goal and define it clearly. This will create a self-driven environment which is not only productive but one that also reduces expensive hustles in supervising and snoopy guidance to irresponsible individuals.

Authenticity encourages practicality. With practicality, people are able to pragmatically link the issues at hand with the situation on the ground. No matter how serious attention your objectives need, it is wise to look out of the box and relate the matter at hand with current issues that many can identify with, and this will include the political and economic perspectives of the day. Any steps taken towards solving any problem are out of touch and are as useless as deodorized dog-shit.

The level of your authenticity will clearly define your knowledge too, so get your proof and supporting evidence from trusted resources, and where possible, have it as your original idea.

These make you reliable, and stand out in a crowd of copycats. As such, being authentic helps you expand your field of knowledge. When people face hardships, they are forced to think beyond the box and thus expand their intelligence antennae and thus impart more knowledge upon themselves. Since they are not willing to just borrow leaves carelessly, they embark on painstaking research in a bid to come up with novel solutions to emerging problems.

Authenticity motivates transparency. A leader who is authentic in his leadership has nothing to hide. And yes, you should have nothing to hide, get your ego out there and put across your message in the best way that suits you and your subordinates. Let your directions lead others, have your voice acted upon and let yourself be the best you've always wanted to be.

Chapter 8: Ethical leadership

Doing the Right Thing

Ethical leadership is important. You can imagine being led by a leader who lacks commendable ethics. Leadership is only for those who have the ability to present themselves as role models to the rest. If you can't be an epitome of irreproachable ethics, then you have no business leading. As such, this piece explores the profound benefits of being an ethical leader.

To begin with, an ethical leader who practices impregnable ethics is able to command the respect of their followers. It is impossible to people who do not hold you in high esteem. The reason why any leader receives the unquestionable respect of their subordinates is because they sought to lead by example. It would be myopic to hope to win the respect of those under you if you have not shown respect to them by upholding the requisite painstaking ethics.

Again, being an ethical leader helps one understand the feeling of those under them. By choosing to be ethical yourself and understanding your subordinates makes you inspire a sense of motivation. With followers who feel appreciated and understood, the leader has a better chance to rule and lead with grace. The reward of understanding those under you is having them understand you as well. And any leader should be happy having subordinates who understand him.

Thirdly, an ethical leader is able to cultivate friendship with their subordinates. Psychologists have shown that people are naturally rebellious and they easily may choose to disobey while knowing that they will be punished anyway. However, they have been able to show that it is not easy for people to wrong their friends. The punishment brought by breaking the law is not as deterrent as the mental guilt of wronging a friend. With this, they have succeeded in proving that the best way to win the obedience is becoming their friends.

Lastly, an ethical leader is able to create an atmosphere of camaraderie. When the boss loves and appreciates all those under them, they motivate them to love and become better friends among themselves. The opposite is quite true. A leader who does not love and appreciate their employees causes strife among them and makes them start treating each other with contempt and suspicion.

Define your organization's value

To lead people with character and integrity, you must set an example. You are the leader, remember? And your team follows you because you represent that authority and integrity they need in order to guide their actions. First, you need to understand yourself, your own values as well as the organization's values.

As an example, the global technology giant 3M is famous for its company values.

Why? Because the team–from top executive managers to the mailroom– live for the concepts of honesty and integrity every day. 3M defines clearly that it expects staff to keep promises, have personal accountability and respects others in the workforce. Every leader knows this and works following these rules. As a result, everyone else follows.

As a leader, it is your duty to set rules and codes and to make sure that you enforce them.

Your personal values are very important in your work as a leader because you can define what's most important in your life. Your values should determine your priorities and, deep down, they probably are the measures you use to determine if your life is turning out the way you want to.

Their absence brings ambiguity and can be a real source of unhappiness.

That's why you need to make a conscious effort to identify your values and their importance.

How Values Help You

Values exist even if we don't recognize them or we don't accept them. When you manage to acknowledge them, your life catches that shapes you dreamt. Making plans and taking decisions become easier. Questions like these will definitely help you to make decisions in life:

- *What job should I pursue?*

- *Should I accept this promotion?*

- *Should I start my new business?*

- *Should I compromise, or be form with my position?*

- *Should I follow tradition or travel down a new path?*

You have the answer and it will help you understand your real priorities and you will be able to take the right direction and accomplish your life goals.

In conclusion, a leader who aspires to present a strong ethical personality motivates their followers to be ethical as well. With this transparency, accountability, and integrity sweep across the entire organization.

Chapter 9: Perceiving the true meaning of power

Power is the ability to influence others towards accomplishing a certain goal. The ability of a leader to influence the activities of others is what may be defined as power. Leadership is based on power without which it cannot exist.

Position power is one described by the job title where one works. It is vested in a leader by the organization to exercise it on behalf of the administrators.

A different form of power is personal power. It is power vested in a leader by other people. It is an indication of the commitment the subordinates have towards their leader. It is followed and strengthened by the people's belief that the leader has the legitimacy to give them instructions that they will eventually follow.

When a leader possesses qualities that followers admire, is created referent power. Followers maybe noticed trying to imitate or copy their leader in various ways. Referent power varies from one leader to another.

Some wield influence over a small number of people, while others have admiration from over millions, through their charisma and personality.

Leaders have various forms of wielding power. There are those who exercise their power over others when they don't do what is required of them. They impose penalties on such individuals, taking various forms ranging from verbal abuse, demotion from job position or even withdrawal of privileges.

In the above case, the followers believe that the leader is capable of imposing a penalty of his choice to the subjects. For it to be effective, it must be something that the followers do not enjoy going through. It should be a penalty that affects the targeted follower directly, for example, a ban on tobacco will not affect a non-smoker.

When a leader makes it a routine to reward his subjects when they meet his expectations, he tends to wield some degree of power over them. They always do things the best way possible so that they may be rewarded at the end of the task.

As such, it must be a reward that is appealing to the followers for them to view it as an incentive. For the leader to be perceived as powerful, he must be dependable. He must be someone who fulfills his promise.

It is crucial that the reward offered is proportionate to the task the subject has completed. If the reward is way smaller than the task completed, the subject may feel undervalued. Good leaders know how to build power around their followers. They do not need to command it but rather comes out on its own.

Chapter 10: Emotional intelligence is a binder between leadership and coaching

Many people may have an understanding of other forms of intelligence, but they may not be quite familiar with emotional intelligence. Emotional intelligence is a pivotal ingredient that every accomplished leader should have. As such, this article explores the importance and definition of emotional intelligence in leadership and leadership coaching.

Emotional intelligence is the ability to manage your own emotions and those of others. It includes three major skills. The first one is the kind of emotional awareness that identifies one's emotions and those of others. The second aspect involves the ability to harness your emotions and those of others and applying them to solving the problems at hand. The third aspect is about regulating your own emotions and also the knack to help others handle their emotions.

With that said, how does emotional intelligence act as the binder between leadership and coaching? To begin with, a leader and coach who are able to identify their own emotions are in an excellent position to take the necessary steps to act on them. For instance, a leader/coach who knows that they are tempered will not let their temper ruin their good influence on their subordinates/trainees. Any coach/leader that has an emotional awareness of their negative emotions will rule them and enhance the coach-trainee relationship for better results.

Further, a leader/coach who

understands and is able to identify the emotions of others is able to handle them in a way that does not motivate the undesirable emotions in them. Even when the negative emotions emerge in a particular subordinate or trainee, the coach/leader who is emotionally intelligence will know how to take control of the situation. During the coaching process, the trainees have to be taught the importance of emotional intelligence in leadership. Since it is impossible for anyone to teach what they do not know, it is imperative that the coaches themselves understand what emotional intelligence is way before they start coaching others about it.

Finally, we all know how emotions affect the way we respond to situations. Any seasoned leader/coach knows when to apply the prevailing emotional climate in order to achieve helpful milestones. Some regrettable emotional blunders may sometimes happen. Instead of blaming hell for such developments, any good leader takes charge of the situation and converts the weakness into strength. For instance, when everyone is bitter because things have gone terribly wrong, it is not the time for blame-gaming but the best time to address the underlying triggers of the problem in order to thwart any chances of its future occurrence, and any qualified leader knows this.

Chapter 11: Adaptability is a crucial skill for an agile leader and the key to coaching

Any agile leader must be adaptable and should be able to make their followers adaptable as well. However, it is not easy to achieve adaptability. As such, this piece explores some benefits and tips of being an adaptable leader.

To begin with, a leader who is adaptable should be able to listen and understand those they lead. The whole rationale behind enhancing one's adaptability as a leader is about studying the disposition of the people they are leading and do several adjustments in order to reach them better.

It is said that you should behave like a Roman when you go to Rome. The greatest advantage of leading people that you know and adapt yourself to the peculiar situation at hand is that you are able to avoid some obvious pitfalls that would have otherwise remained obscure. It does not save time but money as well. Interacting with the people you lead in an attempt to know them also cultivates friendship and a sense of camaraderie.

Further, an adaptable leader should be able to domesticate ideas and policies. Despite which leadership school you attended and whatever lofty ideologies you learned there, you should be able to domesticate the leadership ideas you learned in school. The advantage of domesticating your ideas is that it achieves better results. Since little goes to waste in terms of resources and time, money and power are markedly saved.

Adaptable leaders also have the capacity to draw from their wealth of experience and take charge of the situation at hand. There is a famous saying that history has an invariable tendency to repeat itself. As such, whatever happens in a particular situation has probably happened in another. An adaptable leader can thus relate a present crisis with another that happened in the past and borrow a leaf from the past.

The beauty of being a visionary and adaptable leader is that nothing is ever beyond your control as a leader. Another benefit is that originality takes center stage. Adaptable leaders do not follow rigidly set steps for solving a problem. They pragmatically go to the ground and try to substantiate the facts as they are. Armed with these facts, they are full able to engineer real-time solutions that make sense. On the other hand, leaders who have poor adaptability are unable to get themselves habituated to the present crisis and they tend to continue advancing ideas that do not work. This only leads to one big failure to another.

Chapter 12: The power of trust and developing self-awareness

A popular adage ordains that trust is like virginity, once it is broken it cannot be broken it cannot be re-acquired. As such, it pays handsomely to engineer trust in all our dealings with other people. Those that have experienced the tremendous benefits will do anything to cement and maintain it.

In the same vein, self-awareness is as important as one's life. A person who has a high sense of self-awareness knows itself and does not need to rely on the other sources to know who they really are. Contrariwise, people who lack self-knowledge are like a sea vessel that is being buffeted from one end of the ocean to the other by wild tempestuous winds.

As such, this article underscores the importance of trust and self-awareness. Read on to discover why a leader should have these two.

The Power Of trust

Trust is so powerful. It is especially so crucial to a leader than any other person. To begin with, a leader who enjoys the trust of those below him has their respect. Since a leader should have the ability to see ahead of the pack and put in place some sound mechanisms to boost preparedness, they need to have the trust of the followers so that they can accept to follow them. The followers cannot see the future as clearly as the leader. As such, they do not know what should be done to prepare for that future. The leader knows what should be done. For the subordinates to accept what the leader tells them, they have to have the feeling that the leader is acting in their best interests as well as those of the organization.

The Essence of Developing Self-Awareness

Having underscored the importance of self-awareness in the second paragraph, it is important to note that self-awareness does not happen in an instance, it is developed. Therefore, a leader should have a lofty sense of self-knowledge just like the followers should. However, a leader who does not know himself cannot help the subordinates to discover themselves. Although long, any leader worth the name must be willing to embark on the arduous journey of self-discovery. Set off, by asking yourself: "What are my strengths?" Then, "What are my weak points?"

Note that your weaknesses are as important as your strengths. As such, you must not be a narcissistic perfectionist who decidedly blinds his eyes on their weaknesses. Our weaknesses are just as important as our strong points. Know them!

Chapter 13: Coaching leadership style

Leadership may be described as process or ability to motivate or direct others. When a manager is working as a coach, he is certainly helping those whom he works with to improve their skills and performance at work.

There are many times when we analyze our performance track we realize that there exist gaps in willpower and self-discipline that end up holding us back. High-performance coaching helps people identify and explore their motivation and overcome the blockers that deter them from achieving progress in the activities they are involved in.

Featuring this, evidence galore has shown that people with long term goals end up being successful than those without. There are many times when one is seen as primarily a holder of a position like that of a manager, but also to be seen as a leader; one who offers genuine inspiration and clear guidance. One needs to navigate through these roles tactfully in order to achieve an intellectual distinction in his/her company or even at the workplace.

There is an ultimate need for one to quit habitual moves and instead embrace relearning basic skills in the right way. This creates a calm atmosphere for self-development in leadership. Some life's setbacks tend to prevent one from achieving their set goals. High-performance training is very effective in dealing with such occurrences of stress and burnout in life.

Depending on our perceived difficulty of challenges, this model shows the emotional state that one is likely to experience when trying to accomplish various tasks. One of the aims of the coach should be helping the learner get confident with the skills needed to achieve his goals in life or in a set duration of time.

Some fears are a reality while others are just a mind-play of negative tricks on us to be safe. A coach needs to take some time to deal with a trainee's fear of situations or action. Once he identifies them and discusses them, the power in them is broken and weakened. Still, a coach needs to take face the eventualities of life with the courage to avoid distress.

When one is unable to accomplish tasks repeatedly, a tendency to feel guilt may overcome one and may actually kill their morale to do things. Some people get afraid of virtually everything and have little ability to overcome their worries. Coaches can help such individuals by openly discussing their worries which end up weakening the impact they cause to the trainees.

High-performance coaching not only challenges the trainees but also supports them in developing the levels they are able to attain a happy and successful career.

Chapter 14: Coaching as a meta-profession

Leadership coaching has become necessary in various fields of management. Workforce needs to be equipped with skills that will enhance their output as well as their interaction with one another at the workplace. Resources to be used for training by the coach are very vital. They should be carefully picked in order to ensure the set goals that have been achieved. A framework needs to be set up such that to be able to evaluate oneself with the progress the coaches are making. A physical therapy with pre-requisite training technique uses the latest principles of coaching. This should be aimed at mentoring to upgrade posture through body awareness.

Efficient tools of coaching that revolve around guidance, support and strategies that help create a conducive environment and to improve the perception of learners are of a mandatory importance. In the event that a manager gets concerned by a demotivated workforce, sometimes a pay rise may not be the solution but rather coaching the workforce on social techniques that they need to employ while with each other. Teamwork is number one if outstanding results are part of the expectations in any organization. In the coaching process, coaches need to identify forms of self-limiting decisions resourceful emotions and sometimes beliefs that tend to disfigure the focus of an individual in their struggle to accomplishing their goals.

It takes real hard work to become what we want or rather what we ought to be. This is largely contributed by the fact that we are all born into an unsympathetic world where success is hardly won. Self-empowerment coupled with personal development and a general coaching education is a mandatory ingredient in the success recipe.

Consultations are in most cases a positive input to effective management and in other cases to improve the existing quality of output. Organizational development and professional leadership are the most important aspects of the practice and theory of management.

Upcoming coaches need to re-evaluate themselves by observing how more experienced coaches carry out themselves. Coaching is a very sensitive profession as one needs to carry him/herself with care to avoid killing the dream or the morale of a coach. Once one goes through these induction activities, they develop collective understanding and share in the meanings of different occupation culture as the coaching goes on. As time goes, the coach is able to identify key areas that need more emphasis in their coaches so that they are able to disseminate the same knowledge to their workforce or target group.

Chapter 15: Golden rules of coaching

Leadership coaching does not just go about lectures. It entails much more than that. First, one needs to identify the problem but rather to coach the person so that their skills to handle the problem and similar ones that may arise in future are enhanced. For the real power to be brought out vividly, it needs to come from deep within for it to bring sustainable change.

The coach needs to be at the service of the client. The coach needs to put his ego aside and listen and sometimes silence the client, be direct and supportive. A little play and some rudeness may also be blended well so that it breaks the monotony of the topic at hand.

The choices we make are far more reaching than we sometimes think. Things people say or do and sometimes the emotions expressed sometimes say much more about ourselves. Coaching clients makes them open up only to realize that they are even more resourceful than and with the resources around them. This helps them to accomplish their visions and goals. Challenges start becoming possibilities.

Clients need to struck with a sense of humor to make them get to the creative side of their brains. Playfulness and stillness help the coach get to their own focus too. Effective coaching revolves around aspects such as shaping the future. The future should not only be envisioned but also created. Ideas need to be tested against existing resources.

Making things happen is a leader's number one priority. They must have a way of converting strategies into action. An effective leader knows how to assign accountability and which decisions to manage and which to delegate and ensuring teamwork in the process.

Any leader looks forward to optimizing his team's performance. This can only be achieved by bringing out the best in the people. Talent must be built and engaged for immediate results to be achieved. Building the next generation is a key aspect of leadership. People, competence and human-capital developers are required for strategic success in the future.

Investing in oneself is the key to the leadership model one wants to offer. A leader cannot influence others unless he has created time and energy in self-awareness enhancement of personal attributes that will go hand-in-hand with what the followers expect of him. An effective leader is pace-setting, participative, affiliative and visionary. However leaders have different preferred styles of leadership, blending both soft and hard approaches, yet blending the two in the management of tasks and caring for peoples' concerns.

Chapter 16: The power of coaching

Coaching people in leadership is not an easy venture. It is tantamount to being a teacher in which case one has to know what they are teaching before they stand before the learners. Read on to discover a few tips that are going to help you as you embark on leadership coaching.

One of the surefire tips to guide when doing leadership coaching is engaging all the parties involved. You must desist from engaging in an endless monologue that does not seek to incorporate all the parties involved. If you cannot succeed in getting all the participants while coaching, then you better stop doing it. Ensure that the whole team is alert and motivated. This means that the person doing the coaching should be a savvy mind that can detect when some team members are withdrawn or left out.

Moreover, a leadership coach has to be as practical as possible. Note that all the people you are coaching spent a lot of time in school and they, therefore, have no interest in being subjecting to the rigmaroles of formal class work. You should always begin by being as practically motivational as possible. Right from the start underscore the benefits of the coaching and the kind of helpful skills the trainees are going to have at the end of the session. By making the process as informal as possible and fun oriented, you are going to doubtless win the attention and goodwill of the learners.

Quote examples of prosperous people the learners are familiar with and ones who have benefited from similar coaching. This gives them a mental image of how they are going to be once they complete the coaching session. You may also elucidate how you have benefited from similar tutorials in the past and how they fundamentally changed your life. This makes those being coached plucked the requisite morale to continue with the coaching process. Again, it makes them take the whole undertaking positively, leading to better results.

Finally, you should drop any schoolmasterly attitude toward the people you are coaching. Being already a leader yourself, you must teach others how to mingle with other people gracefully. Make it a platform for equal participation. Ask questions and challenge your audience to offer practical answers. You must try to avoid imposing your opinions on your trainees. Make the session trainee-oriented since it is not you learning but them. Encourage authenticity and originality throughout the whole process.

Chapter 17: The foundation of Coaching

"Maybe this year, we ought to walk through the rooms of our lives not looking for flaws, but looking for potential."

Business environment is changing radically and rapidly and it will continue this process. The old methods used by managers and leaders to upgrade people's mentality and the entire organization are no longer effective. For achieving a competitive advantage, companies must customize new approaches to reach, inspire and keep the new employees. Coaching was meant for this...Coaching can unveil potential, maximize performance and contribute to a corporate culture congruent with the new era.

Coaching has become a critical tool for organizational changes. Change is seen as fundamental for organizations to develop and adjust to today's swiftly shifting marketplace. But people and organizations are still very resistant and reticent to change.

Coaching is the key of withdrawing the impact of change in people and organizations perspective. It can facilitate a productive shift in persons, teams and systems by empowering leaders, managers and employees to unveil their potential that otherwise might go unexplored.

The traditional hierarchical model of leading and influencing is no longer recommended for thriving in today's intricate and dynamic marketplace and many organizations have become aware of this. To embrace more relational, collaborative and consultative model for leading and influencing, organizations has developed a new culture, the one of coaching, that embolden organizational adaptability and learning and it came in sight as the best manner of helping individuals to gain knowledge, to learn to think and work together effectively.

Professional coaching is an unceasing relationship which focuses on helping you clarify vision, beliefs and values and taking action toward the realization of your goals and desires. It uses the process of investigation and personal discovery to create your level of awareness and responsibility and ensures you encouragement, structure, and feedback. In other words, it uses your questions and answers to analyze the aspects of your entire life and as an effect of its impact, it will increase the level of personally and professionally accomplishment.

Many people don't know the difference between coaching and therapy because both of them are very powerful and effective fields that have the same purpose-to help people. Therapy is based on past issues and the asking why questions, focusing on solving those problems of the clients, while coaching concentrates on the clients creating action from their present situation and the asking of how questions.

Coaching is meant for everyone but is not for everyone, because individuals have to be ready and willing to change. A person is ready for coaching when he is willing to start a relationship based on mutual trust, competent to find where he is and what he want and longing to take action.

This process starts with clarifying the present outlook, values, engagements, goals, skills and life balance.

Chapter 18: The benefits of coaching and how to be a coach

Professional coaching brings many marvelous benefits for people and implicitly for companies because people are the most important resource of a company. It brings new and up-to-date perspectives, personal and vocation challenges, enhanced decision-making competences, greater neutral effectiveness, increased confidence. Studies have shown that people trying coaching can expect substantial development in productivity, satisfaction not only in work but also in life and fulfillment of significant goals.

Increased Productivity

Coaching can increase the level of productivity by uncovering the human potential and unlocking the latent sources of creativity, inspiration and knowledge. It is a great tool to boost the confidence of an employee, maintain the professional development and build a brand name for an employee interested in self-growth.

Coaching will facilitate the

acquirement of new skills quicker, more efficiently than a basic training, support retention and build a team based on performance as an indispensable value.

Many employees start this process because of the lack of confidence in their aptitudes and performance, the reason of holding them back, and they expect an imposing positive impact after the coaching training.

Coaching is not based on providing advice, but the chance given to the manager to act as a leader for its team group, supporting them to raise worries and preoccupations and find solutions on their own for every challenge. The fundamental role of the coach is to help driving the discussions through active listening.

The role of active listening is to involve everyone in conversation and develop people mind and creativity, because after a relative short time, they will be able to accept positions of responsibility, which will bring job satisfaction, confidence, and a strong desire to work for performance, which in turn builds productivity.

Positive People

Organization requirements can be accomplished only boosting the confidence of employees in order to face the multitude of challenges that arises every day.

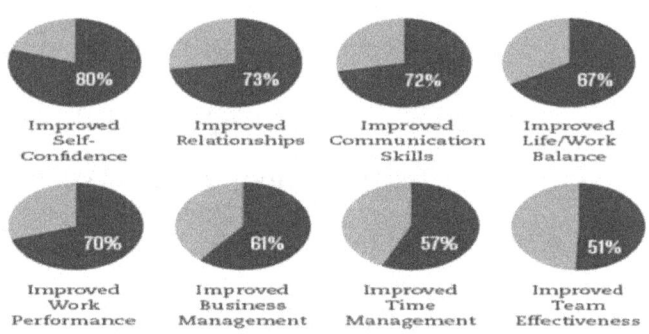

Return on Investments

Measurable outcomes are generated from true commitments for excellence which are provided by the clarity and the amount of learning from the coaching process. Big companies declare that from the process of coaching you can at least take your investment back. But the benefits are enormous and you can see them on a long-term.

Satisfied Clients

Companies and individuals who hire a coach are very satisfied with the benefits because this process involves a genuine discovery of the problems and an answer to it, maximization of individual strengths, overcome personal barriers, achievement of new skills and competencies, preparation for new and challenging obstacles, growing of potential through continuous learning, capacity of managing themselves and action in order to achieve high performance in personal goals.

Improves the process of decision-making

Coaching is also a process that helps

individuals to take their own decisions, without any job expectation and constraints. This will make them bear out their own path, within the purpose of their own responsibilities. The contribution of the coach stands in encouraging and turning people into champions, without the fear of failure.

In conclusion, coaches need to understand that their people are creative, resourceful and productive. Coaching is not about fixing people, it is about helping people to discover the inner strength and motivation they have always had inside. It is about finding the true potential within people by spending a lot of time asking questions.

Chapter 19: The grow model -why do we need to be a leader to coach people?

It is a pipe dream to hope to lead others when you are not a leader yourself. It is like teaching Greek to other people if you do not know it yourself. As such it pays to master your craft first before you can start teaching it to others. Therefore, this piece underscores some aspects of true leadership that those acting as leadership coaches must acquaint themselves with. Read on to discover more.

A true coach needs to be a leader who teaches their trainees to outline their leadership goals. Setting clear goals while everyone is groping in the darkness is the very acme of good leadership and anyone coaching people on leadership must be very familiar with this. With this knowledge and ability, they will be able to motivate their trainees to have the same abilities.

A true leader who qualifies to be coach needs to have a clear vision to see the future and also one who has eyes for the current situation. This is because the future cannot exist without today because the present moment is a bridge of the future. Those learning useful leadership tips must familiarize themselves with this aspect of leadership. As such, only a seasoned leader who has perfected the art of deciphering the present moment will have the adroitness to lead others. A leadership coach must, therefore, be a qualified leader for himself.

A true leader and coach must teach his trainers that every good leader must always consider all the options at their disposal when tackling a problem. For the trainees to understand how a qualified leader weighs up a situation and comes up with options on how to get out of the mayhem, they ought to be taught by a chartered leader who has practically done it before.

Further, any leadership coach must be himself a good leader who underscores the essence of a strong will. How can one coach others to have a strong will when leading while they have not practiced it before himself? Yes, a leadership coach must be a leader who has used strong will in their past positions of leadership.

Finally, any leadership coach must be himself a leader who understands the essence of charting out the way forward despite how gloomy this look. So how can you tell people to always come up with a way forward while in a crisis while you have not done it yourself? A leader must be a doyen in the field who has practically implemented the skills they teach.

Chapter 20: The GROW Model

A simple process for Coaching

The GROW Coaching model is the best well-appreciated coaching framework in the world. There are dozens of methods of coaching in this world, and many of them, which are excellent tools, are only facilitators of learning rather than letting you direct it. This marvelous tool was conceived by Graham Alexander and it was perfected by John Whitmore.

Unlike other coaching models, the GROW model is much more than a toolbox linked to an acronym, it is an extraordinary approach which will help individuals to convert their potential into the height level of performance. I think this is the simple reason of its wonder-working success.

The essence of high-performance coaching

You can achieve performance and limited success using the GROW coaching model, but without understanding the philosophy that stands behind this coaching approach, you will become confused about what is truly possible. The quintessence of good coaching is all about you, the power you have to help your coachee to increase awareness and take responsibility. The process of coaching is very important also because it brings structure to the conversation, but this is not the main idea of coaching. Creating consciousness and responsibility are. Build the coaching session in the context of awareness and responsibility and it will take the turn for the better drastically.

The 4 elements of the GROW Coaching Model

The GROW coaching model provides the coach an undemanding, yet powerful, framework. The coaching model designed by Whitmore has 4 steps. The conversation can start at any one of this four steps of the GROW Model and the coachee might begin by telling you information about something s/he wants to accomplish (GOAL), present problems (Reality), a new idea for improving a situation (Options) or by defining an action plan (Will).

Each question you address to the coachee should aim to increase consciousness and responsibility. It is the mixture of context and sequence, along a lot of practice, which will make you become an excellent coach.

Step 1. The Grow model: G for Goal setting

The most important part of the first coaching step is to determine and agree upon one or more goals that the coachee wants to accomplish. The ideal situation is to define a comprehensible goal for the coaching session itself and a long-term performance goal.

It is essential to give value and direction to your conversation with the coachee, to make sure s/he knows the reason for the conversation and the objectives of it.

Individual objective setting is not only a fundamental stage for great coaching but for Strategy Execution in general. Goal setting is one of the most over-elaborate elements in organizational science. To become a great coach means more than being a master of SMART goals, but having a solid understanding of the topic.

Effective questioning is a key element of the performance coaching.

I prepared you 15 questions you can use during the Goal Setting phase:

1. *What is the purpose of the discussion?*

2. *What should happen to you during this conversation to walk away*

feeling that this time was well spent?

3. If I could grant you a wish for this session, what would it be?

4. What outcome would you like to achieve from this session/discussion?

5. What would you like to happen that is not happening now or what you would like not to happen that is happening now?

6. Thinking about the outcome you want to achieve, can we do that in the time we have available?

7. What do you want to achieve on

long-term?

8. *Can you describe success? What does it look like?*

9. *How would you describe the level of control or influence you have over your goals?*

10. *What would be a landmark on the way?*

11. *When do you want to accomplish it by?*

12. *Is that realistic?*

13. *Is that positive, challenging, attainable?*

14. *Will it be of real value for you?*

15. How will you measure it?

These questions will develop the sense of awareness and responsibility.

Step2. The gRow model: R for Reality

The current situation can be analyzed only with objectivity. Most people think they are objective, but the reality reflects another thing. Nobody is. The perfect objectivity doesn't exist. We can only have limited objectivity. There are a lot of aspects that can and will overshadow you, and your coachee's objectivity like expectations, fears, prejudices and different opinions.

But the more we chase to be objective, the more we will be. It is your challenge to accede as possible to reality, overcoming the mental obstacles. As a coach, you have the mission to help your coachee to remove the false assumptions as possible. Try to find answers to the coachee problem by asking him/her to describe their current reality. This is a fundamental step in solving a problem, because many of us try to solve a problem without having a full understanding of what caused the problem, what was the starting point, and they are missing some of the information they needed to solve the problem effectively. When your coachee starts to tell you his problem, the solution of it starts to reveal itself.

Here are 15 questions you can use during your second coaching phase which is about reality:

1. *What is happening now? (where, when, what, who, how much, how often). Try to describe everything.*

2. *How do you know that this is precise/ accurate?*

3. How would you verify or how can you verify that this is true?

4. What other aspects/ factors are relevant?

5. Who is part of it?(directly and indirectly)

6. What is your perception?

7. When things are going badly on this issue, what happens to you?

8. What happens to the others directly involved in this problem?

9. What is the effect of others?

10. What have you done to solve this problem?

11. What results did that produce?

12. What is missing in this situation?

13. What do you have that you're not using?

14. What is holding you back?

15. What is really going on? (intuition)

Step3. The grOw model: O for Options

Once you are your coachee have discovered the current reality, it's time to find out and understand what is possible–potential options, behavior or decisions that can lead to a decisive solution.

Help your coachee to create a long list because your objective during this stage is not to find the right answer, but to enlighten your coachee and help him identify different ideas and solutions. You want to exclude from the session obstacles like preferences, the need for completeness or feasibility that can block the brainstorming process. Remember that the real value is given by creativity.

In this stage, you have to focus on the quantity of ideas and solutions rather than their quality and feasibility. In the next stage you will choose one from that long list of creative possibilities.

Here are some example questions for this stage:

1. *How could you do to change the situation?*

2. *Tell me what options for action you see. Do not worry whether they are realistic at this stage.*

3. *What approach/actions have you seen used, or used yourself, in similar circumstances?*

4. *What else could you do?*

5. *What if...? (time, money, power?)*

6. *Who might be able to help?*

7. *Would you like to hear another suggestion from me?*

8. *Which option do you prefer the most?*

9. *What are the benefits and costs of each?*

10. *Which options are of interest to you?*

11. *Would you like to choose an option to work on?*

Step 4: The groW model: W for Will

The aim of the last phase is to convert a discussion into a decision, using the outcome of the three previous coaching stages. You will guide you coachee to answer to another set of questions.

By analyzing the current Reality and Options, your coachee will understand how s/he can accomplish the great goal. This is amazing, but without help in driving the future actions, it has no value. That's why you need to help your coachee to take responsibility and commit to action. To maximize the chances of success, you need to take into consideration any potential

obstacles, find ways to overcome them
and agree on the resources needed.

In this stage the coachee has to make
several decisions, this means that his
decision can be to take no action at all.
The coachee always maintains choice
and ownership.

Here are some inspiring questions for
the last stage of the coaching
model-Will:

1. *What option or options do you
   choose?*

2. *To what extent does this meet all
   your objectives?*

3. *What are your criteria and*

quantifications for success?

4. When precisely are you going to start and finish each action step?

5. What could arise to cloud you in taking these steps?

6. What personal resistance do you have, if any, to taking these steps?

7. What will you do to eliminate these external and internal factors?

8. Who needs to know what your plans are?

9. What support do you need and from whom?

10. What will you do to obtain that

support and when?

11. *What could I do to support you?*

12. *What commitment on a 1-to-10 scale do you have to taking these agreed actions?*

13. *What prevents this from being a 10?*

14. *What could you do or alter to raise this commitment closer to 10?*

15. *Is there anything else you want to talk about now or are we finished?*

Chapter 21: Developing a Coaching Culture to Increase Productivity by Improving Relationships

Coaching is an outstanding management tool to increase individual performance, deal with areas of development and enhance productivity.

Before starting the process of coaching, you should make your team understand what you expect from them and this happens when it is provided a regular performance feedback. When the process starts, coaching has the purpose of developing skills and knowledge in order to build on the job performance.

Teams are the engine of an organization, they are the force that drives most of the companies to success.

The success of a team, no matter if it's a functional team, a team of managers or a project team, is reflected when people work together effectively. So when the members of a team don't work very well together, the performance and the productivity can suffer. The symptoms of an unhealthy team can be discovered in their hostility, conflicting goals, and unclear expectations. In order to avoid these effects, you need to be proactive about straightening your team performance.

Even when a team is meeting its objectives, there is always space for improvement.

If you're struggling to find the answer to how you can help your team improve, there is only an answer: with a good team coaching which is very different from individual coaching. It is an essential tool for management and leadership and it can take your team to the next level.

Team coaching

Team coaching helps people understand how to work effectively together. It is an efficient method that will reduce conflict and improve their working relationships so that they can focus on achieving objectives.

For coaching a team, you have to focus on interpersonal skills and interactions because from the way people act with their teammates and the way they interact you can understand where is the rupture and work on concealing it.

People must learn how to work together and understand how to relate to one another. Otherwise the team outcome will be affected.

Understanding Team Dynamics

Understanding the dynamics of a team is the start for an effective team coaching. In this process, you analyze the way team members relate to one another. The difference in styles of working and communicating between people can create barriers. When we find a person with a different style from our own, we often get frustrated with that person and we fail to recognize his/her strengths.

Personality and behavior evaluation are great tools for improving the team performance and giving team members a better understanding of why they react in certain ways to their teammates.

This new approach will help them think about how they can relate to one another more effectively and it will raise the level of tolerance between people. They have to understand that different ideas may be valid in different situations.

Myers-Briggs Personality Test is a great tool for unveiling the individual pattern in aspects as communication and conflict resolution.

In every company, you can see people who just can't seem to get along or people who seem to live in parallel universes because they can't communicate with others. The solution is to identify their personality types and understand the differences between one-another. It will increase the harmony from the team. Each person is unique, but personality theorists believe that we have certain common aspects that group us into personality types. Knowing your personality type, you can understand your reactions and control them in case they pull you back or destroy relationships. Recognizing your teammates' types can improve your understanding and appreciation towards them and also can help you get along better with them.

The Myers-Briggs Type Indicator is one of the best well-known personality tests.

It has four psychological scales:

1. [E]xtraversion –[In]troversion

It is related to our energy flow.

- Extroverts are stimulated and motivated by external events and people, they are very talkative, showing their feelings and working well in groups.

- Introverts hide their feelings, prefer to work alone and learn by themselves; they also prefer self-examination and discovery.

2. [S]ensing-[IN]tuition

It is related to the way we learn information.

- Sensing individuals use their five senses – sight, hearing, touch, taste and smell – to understand the world. They like examples from the real life, they are very practical and get the facts while possibly missing the main idea.

- Intuitive people depend on instincts. Their work is based on hunches and feelings, using their imagination to the maximum and getting the main idea while missing some of the facts.

3. [T]hinking-[F]eeling

This is how we take decisions.

- The logic and objective criteria are the tools of thinking people. "Why" is their favorite question and they like debates.

- Feeling people rely on values and subjectivity. They like harmony, agreement and helping others.

4. [J]udging-[P]erceiving

This is about the way we deal with the world.

- Judging people are purposeful and

they like structure, plans, and rules.

- Perceiving people take an easygoing, relaxed approach. They are very flexible, open to change and they like to explore.

Determining Personality Type

To identify each type of personality, this tool uses 16 different typologies, based on which part of each scale is dominant. A person who prefers Introversion, Sensing, Thinking, Judging will be a ISTJ and the has a certain set of personal characteristics associated with this type.

ISTJ are serious, practical, quiet and dependable. They are very responsible, accomplished and determined. They work accurately, handle high-pressure situations calmly, but they tend to take quick and impulsive decisions. They may be impatient and forget to appreciate someone else's work. They can be an accountant, corrections supervisors, doctor, engineer, manager, technical operator.

Don't forget that each person is unique even if they are included in a certain type of personality. They can bring special gifts in the company and they create value. Remember that 100 people with the same type of personality are in their essence unique due to genetics, experiences, interests and other factors, but they have something strong in common.

Knowing your personality type will help you understand yourself better, discover what motivates you and energize you. It also helps you improve relationships and understand someone else behavior without being skeptic or critic. When you meet someone with the same personality type, you can use those information to start a great conversation because you know yourself and you know what to say and how to behave. And you also can prevent fighting with someone who definitely has a different opinion that you.

There is also 360-degree feedback tool that help people understand themselves better. There are aspects of you and your team work performance that are not working very well and parts that work more satisfying than you expected. With a usual performance review, you can see the full picture. You objectivity and judgment is darkened by biases and subjective perspectives. The

360-degree feedback will help you fill the image of your performance.

Using this tool you gather information from the people working with or affected by, the person being evaluated. This will provide an accurate and more complete picture. It will also encourage the teamwork.

Your duty as a coach is to bring team members together to discuss their individual characteristics and help them find the best way to work together. With a bigger level of understanding, team members will see one another differently and they will adjust behaviors in order to get along very well and achieve better results. This will also increase the empathy between them.

Establish Behavior Expectations

The only way to improve relationships is to understand other people's perspectives and respect them. However, teams have to follow ground rules so they can achieve their goals. That's why team coaching is based on developing a strong and clear set of behavior and communication expectations.

The expectations are the base of

empathy and understanding and help ensure that individual preferences had not received more importance than team objectives.

An efficient way to formalize these expectations is to use a team charter in which you highlight the set of behavior rules the team has to follow.

Team Charters-Getting your teams off to a great start

Working in team may be a fantastic experience if your team works well, but if people are pulling in different ways, this experience can be complicated and without many great results. The worse part of this type of experiences is that the team can focus on off target objectives, can fail in using the important resources they should manage cautiously and this will bring to consequences for the company.

The team charter is a map for the team, defining the purpose of it, how member should work together and what outcome they should achieve. This will give a strong sense of direction for the team if it is respected.

The team charter is created when the team is formed, in this way everyone is focused on the right direction from the beginning. It can be also created when the team is in trouble and need help to define the big picture of the goal they work for.

There are seven standard elements that can be adapted to your team situation:

- **Context,** where is described the purpose of team formation, the problem it is trying to solve, why is this problem significant for the organization' objectives and the consequences of the problem in case it is not solved.

I. What problem is being addressed?

II. What result is expected?

III. Why is this important?

- **Mission and Objectives**, where is defined the mission of the team. It is the heart of the charter because, without a mission, people don't know what they have to achieve. Another step is to convert the mission into SMART goals and objectives. This will keep the team on track. The SMART framework is based on specific, measurable, attainable, relevant and time-bound goals, in this way the objectives can be measured and the success of the mission can be monitored.

- **Composition and Roles.** The effectiveness of the teams can be seen when in the team exists members with skills and experienced required for that job, when the members can bring experiences and approached from a wide range of backgrounds, when they have enough members to do the job. Try to find members who can bring outcome to the team and then match the team members to roles, determine gaps in their skills and abilities that are necessary for the team to reach its goals. The most effective way to do this is to list each member and tell him what his role and responsibilities are.

- Who will be the leader of the team?

- Who is the liaison between the team and the other stakeholders?

- Who is responsible for what duties and outcomes?

- Authority and Boundaries. Once you have set the roles of the team, you have to determine what the team member can and can't do to accomplish the mission.

- How much time the team should spend on achieving the mission? What are the priorities?

- How should team members solve the conflicts between their day jobs and the team mission?

- What is the budget of the mission? (time and money)

- Can the team recruit new members in case they can't finish the task in time?

- What can the team member to do and what they can't? What does it need prior approval to do?

- **Resources and Support.** The resources available for accomplishing the goals include budgets, time, equipment and people. They have to be strictly monitored and sometimes for this, the team needs coaching.

- **Operations**. This section outlines how the team will operate every day.

- **Negotiation and Agreement.** The process of negotiation is fundamental for teams. The team's client set up the Context and the Mission, Objectives, composition, roles, boundaries and resources. Then the negotiation between the sponsor, team leader, team and stakeholders take place. Every negotiation needs approval and this is the last process of this stage.

Support Individual Development

Whenever someone from the team is interested in personal development, your duty as a coach is to support this process. The members of a team may need help to learn new skills or improve the old ones, in order to meet the team expectations. You also have to understand the differences between the levels of readiness of each person. Find ways every day to coach the team. Give feedback regularly, help people set individual performance goals.

For every team you have to adapt your coaching approaches because every team is different and the secret of coaching performance stands in your ability as a coach to understand the team members' needs, preferences and styles of work. By helping people to discover their work styles and understand the differences between them, you can work with them to shape behaviors and use their strengths.

This process of improving the performance of a team requires a lot of time and involves a deep look into the team' needs, but the results are well worth it and can also improve the communication and collaboration between members. In one word, they can improve the organization system.

How to provide an effective coaching

1. **Expectations**: Make sure your team expectations have been clearly highlighted and they know what demeanors are expected of them.

2. **Feedback:** Give feedback based on a situation you have perceived.

3. **Measurable outcome**: Set clear steps for improvement with definitely measurable outcomes. You have to

explain how you will monitor and measure every change during the process.

4. **Honesty:** You have to be honest and conduct coaching in person.

5. **Openness:** You have to be very opened to every point of view and opinion and to respect them.

6. **Explanations:** You have to understand and explain the business rationale that stands behind the need for coaching.

7. **Ongoing monitoring**: Finding an effective way to monitor the coaching process will allow you to reach the

behavior change you have planned to
get.

"Coaching is all about having someone
believe in you, about getting valuable
feedback, about seeing things from
new perspectives and setting your
sights on new horizons."

Coaching is the key to improving
productivity in people who are
performing less and develop
techniques for learning and growing.
Creating a coaching culture empire
will establish a positive impact on the
way people perceive coaching.
Coaching should be seen as a positive
opportunity in which they will learn

and grow while they contribute to business triumph.

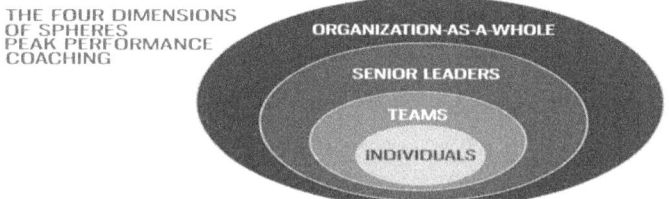

Chapter 22: Coaching for Talent Development

Helping people become more effective

During the economic downturn that started in 2007, which was seen as a global recession, affecting the world markets, many managers have been under pressure to achieve more, but with fewer resources. The difference between those who managed to achieve this goal and those who didn't is the ability to coach their employees in order to increase their productivity and effectiveness.

Another way is to empower them to accept new challenges and responsibilities.

Coaching was the only tool that could solve the problem of some many boundaries from this deficient system.

Coaching revealed the people's ability to develop new skills and assume increased responsibilities, develop their old skills and talents and experiment new ways of doing essential tasks and processes. It also helped the organization by improving harmful attitudes and helping people deal with them, leading people and helping them to solve the problems that blocked their advance, finding the essential problems from the business process and fixing them, helping member of the group to understand the career expectations very well and identifying the issues from the succession planning.

The rapid business change, new performance drivers, the borderless workplace and the new job and career model put a lot of pressure on leadership, which had the purpose to improve strategic role of human resources for competitive edge and performance. It means to leverage the potential of the employees because they are the most important resource a company can have and the success of the company starts with the success of the development of their talents.

The long-term success of a company stands in its ability to change and develop people who work there. Coaching is the key mode to unveil the real potential and maximize its impact on the company goals. The purpose was to convert talent into a strategic priority. Many leaders admitted that their failure was the result of not paying enough attention to the talent strategy:

"What's needed is a deep-rooted conviction, among business unit heads and line leaders, that people really matter that leaders must develop the capabilities of employees, nurture their careers, and manage the performance of individuals and teams".

The ability to build talents in a core competence of the leader and new researches showed there is a huge gap in developing this competence.

This gap is caused by many interrelated issues including:

❖ **Time.** It is the scarcest resource in the world. The poor time management of different leaders brought them to a daily crisis in solving urgent tasks and developing long-term investment in people.

❖ **Focus on visible skills.** New leaders were interested in developing short-time skills rather than building talent, which is less obvious and has a long-term payoff.

❖ **Lack of development culture**. Leaders don't allocate too much time for developing talent because they don't understand that individual coaching and organization coaching can bring value to the company. This is called lack of understanding the motors of every organization or the lack of educational background.

This is why they need to coach people and create a culture of talent development. The GROW coaching model is the key to achieving this goal.

How to do this:

* ❖ **Act as a role model:** Coaches, no matter if they are leaders or managers, need to learn. They have to show how they do this. They will never be more powerful than in the moment they are shown to be learning. Maybe they show vulnerability but they become a model for their coachee.

❖ **Reinforce the value of learning:** Try to explore more than a basic conversation about goals. Use the GROW Model to achieve it.

❖ **Build sustainable processes to support development:** Managers and leaders should coach and develop people. They have to improve areas where is needed and increase the potential of their people.

❖ **Reinforce shared values:** This means that every employee has to link everyday tasks with the values of the company. They have to understand why what they do is important.

❖ **Leverage problems as opportunities for real-world learning and development:** The organization should encourage a business environment where problems are seen as opportunities, not as drawbacks/ obstacles.

Chapter 23: Coaching through Change

Helping people embrace change

Coaching through transition, not just through change

If there is one certain aspect at this moment, it's that there is a lot of change going on.

The world is changing so fast and not even one successful organization can resist too long to this continuous shift without improvement. New products, new services and new ways of working mean that many of us keep learning new skills and adapting to changes in every aspect of life, especially in the workplace.

Every organization is experiencing change, whether it is at large scale, strategic change or small scale change. Change has become a daily life fact.

If there is something that remains constantly uncertain in when the change is going to slow down in pace and when the result of the change will become more certain.

The biggest challenges in an organization are the pace of change and the ambiguity.

Change requires a transition which can influence you at the emotional level and it can be a painful and rocky journey.

"It isn't the change that brings you in, it's the transitions. Change is situational, transition is the psychological process people go through to come to terms with the new situation. Change is external, transition is internal".

Transition and Emotions

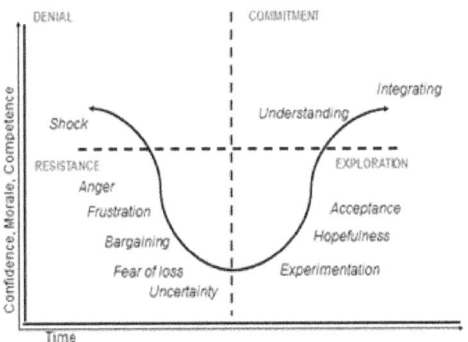

Transition is slow, but change is fast and managers have to face with it in order to deliver efficient results. Change means to accept and embrace the future and forget about the past because it can make you become motionless.

Change management is one of the most useful techniques for

understanding changes and ensures that every change will be smoothly implemented.

The focus of the change is on its impact, especially on individuals, because they are directly affected by change and they have to move from the current situation to the new one. This shift has a strong impact on their life and many of them can't fold on it.

In order to coach people through change and manage it successfully, it is necessary to understand the broad impact of it. Not only the tangible impact has to be considered, but also the personal impact of the individuals affected by it. The Change Curve is the most useful tool that can describe the personal and organizational process of change.

Sponsorship means that there is active sponsorship for change at the executive level of the organization and make sure you engaged the sponsorship to achieve the desired outcome.

Buy-in means that you can count on people affected and involved in change.

Involvement means that you have

the right people working for the implementation of the change.

Impact means to present the consequences of change.

Readiness means to get people ready to accept change, by training, help and providing the right information.

People need to go through the "neutral zone" which is defined by uncertainty, confusion, lack of focus, discomfort and confusion. The potential impact on the organization is decreased productivity, dysfunctional teams and stressed managers and also absenteeism.

There are 3 important reasons why every organizational change fails which derived from the lack of clarity, focus, and direction.

1. **Employee resistance**. They resist change if they don't understand the reason for it and the benefits it can bring to the organization.

2. **Leadership issues**. These issues appear when the leaders can't understand the change and or when they are unclear in how they communicate about it to their teams.

3. Communication is the key to change.

The role of the coach

1. His first mission is to encourage people accept the new situation and see it from a different perspective, with benefits from them.

2. To enable people to explore the feeling of transition, to experience it and then to move on.

3. To make them focus on the results they have to achieve and the steps they need to do every day in order to get there.

4. To help people build their resilience and accept the change.

5. Help people regain the sense of control, focusing on what they can do rather than what they can't.

As a coach, you have the tools and techniques to make people understand why they should respond to the change and implement it. They will learn new skills, gain confidence and become more productive.

There are five principles that are very effective, regardless of the situation and the level in which an individual is involved in an organization.

1. Let the past behind and start learning for the future

Let's take the example of Helen, who was very successful as a manager in IT. She was promoted to a director-level general management, controlling the IT, HR and communications. She gained the recognition of the people from the organization because of her ability to turn teams around and get results. The new challenge was to transform a failing department and make it focus on customers. She was very good in IT, but she hasn't knowledge about the other areas of the organization. The first time when she started taking control, the team said nothing, but soon they questioned her about her knowledge and ability to make decisions about an unknown area. The team started to underestimate her efforts. Soon the morale and the productivity of the team has dipped because they couldn't understand the changes Helen wanted to implement without having the knowledge of it and they didn't support her.

Helen failed because she was unable to understand the new change and face the transition. She didn't make the leap from being a successful IT manager to leading all the areas of the organization. She kept doing and practicing the old techniques and habits she used to implement when she was the IT manager because it made her feel more confident. But the result was the opposite. By not letting go of the past, she lost a tremendous opportunity to succeed as a general manager.

The idea of change is to let the past behind and concentrate on the future. She should have focused on the new position, trying to understand the new responsibilities, preparing her mentally to implement change.

Her error was to think that what had made her successful in the past would bring her the same thing now. New challenges and the fear of being incompetent to face the new changes can impede the learning process.

Someone who is promoted to a higher role because they have succeeded the expectations in a function, like Helen, may find themselves having to learn new skills and knowledge in a short space of time. This process is too fast and the person involved in has to be very productive and conscious of the responsibilities of the new role.

As a coach, you have to question the person in order to help her embrace the change and make sure she knows her duties for the new role:

- What made you successful in your career?

- What are the new skills you need to learn?

- Are there parts of your new job that are critical to success but on which you would prefer not to focus?

- What do you need to ensure that you can make the leap from your old job to the new?

2. Design the strategy that fits the situation and will secure quick wins

Many leaders fail to learn about the new team and fit the strategy to the situation. Each challenge needs a different approach or strategy. As a coach, work through with your coachee to identify the situation and the best strategy that matches it.

It is important to get early wins and get them in the right way because they will help you build credibility in the short term and lay the basis for long-term goals. You need to consider with priority the area that most need attention, as well as those that offer you the greatest chance to improve your performance.

Firstly, you need to focus on building your coachee's personal credibility because early actions influence how people are perceived.

Here are examples of questions you can ask your coachee during the session of coaching through change:

- Which of the four situations are you facing?

- Which of your skills and strengths will be most valuable in this situation?

- Given what you know about the situation, what are the priorities for early wins?

3. Build effective relationships with the boss and your team

The keys for an effective relationship with the boss are the negotiation of success and time spent building the relationship. The first action is to prepare a plan of the goals and actions you want to achieve and to update it regularly with your progress. Another aspect is to present a report of your quick wins to your boss. Responsibility, credibility, and hard work will definitely build a strong relationship with your boss.

As a coach, your responsibility is to support your coachee to take absolute control of making the relationship work, handle expectations from the beginning and clarify requests, negotiate time for achieving your plans, get some quick wins that build credibility for your boss.

When you coach people for creating a strong bond between them and the boss, you should take more time to discover the background of the old relationships with the bosses and also the expectations of each coachee:

- How effectively have you built relationships with new bosses in the past?

- What do you want to say up front?

- How does your new team go with your expectations for performance?

- How do you want your team to operate?

- What do you need to do to support them?

4. **Create a support network and alliances, both internal and external**

One of the mistakes of the new leaders is to focus their influence in a straight line, up to the bosses and down to the employees and they exclude peers and external stakeholders. But sooner they will need the support of people over whom they don't have direct influence. They will need time to create alliances and networks.

The mission of a coach is to encourage the individual to think about the time they have spent building valuable and strong relationships. Make the coachee think about the people who have a critical impact on their success, who are the sources of power that have influence in the organization. Maybe they are people with expertise, recognition, who hold control over the departments and resources or information. As a coach, you have to encourage the leader to talk with others because they can bring value to the leader's initiatives.

- Whose support do you need to succeed?

- What networks are most important to you?

- Who are potential supporters?

5. Support people around you through their transition

There are always people working with the new leaders and this is a great fact because they will benefit from a methodical approach to face the transition. The real challenge after this is to transform the transition into a part of their work.

It is very hard to implement a new approach to an organization, that's why the role of the coach is to guide people to the most effective method.

There are seven steps to an effective

transition:

- Chemistry and first impression are the keys to building relationships and credibility with the clients

- Contracting-setting the manner of working and creating the big image/ direction.

- Diagnostics-create bonds with the stakeholders, understand the block and barriers of any problem. Try to find ways to solve the problems, create a plan.

- High-level design-Create the big-picture vision of the goals you want to achieve and ask stakeholders for support in your plans.

- Detailed design-Choose the most recommended strategy.

- Implementation-Implement your strategy. Be flexible to change.

- Evaluation – Periodically, stop and evaluate your progress and focus first on quick wins that will ensure you credibility and involvement.

Very often people go straight to action and enforce too quickly in the desire to show they can do because quick wins bring credibility.

Throughout our lives, we develop

coping strategies and we use them every day to cope with changes and situations. Changing a job gives us a feeling of insecurity and rummage and we tend to use those coping strategies.

A coach has the duty to make people learn new skills and gain confidence and also to support people to assume influential roles in the organizations.

"Giving people self-confidence is by far the most important thing that I can do. Because then they will act."-Jack Welch

Investing in people means to invest in the quality of your organization because people who work there provide value on your product or services.

"You can have the best strategy and the best building in the world, but if you don't have the hearts and minds of the people who work with you, none of it comes to life".

"An organization's ability to learn, and translate that learning into action rapidly is the ultimate competitive advantage."

Chapter 24: High-performance Coaching

Achieving Full Potential

The mot-a-mot meaning of "high-performance coaching" may seem to be to coach for high performers, in other words, people who are identified as star talents, but high-performance coaching means actually to help people achieve their full potential, in any domain of their lives.

In a company, the idea of high-performance coach means to help people increase their performance at work.

It also means to work with other people within your organization, collaborating with other managers and leaders to make the workplace a high-performance organization, one that gives the opportunity of intensive and efficient development.

The techniques and approaches used

for this type of coaching are borrowed from the military and sports fields, where the performance is the key to success.

The high-performance coaching conversations start with discovering people's visions and ambitions in life. The second step is to find the directions in which people need to move to accomplish their dream and the steps needed for it.

When to use high-performance coaching

The reason why we don't succeed in life is because we have gaps in willpower and self-discipline. This holds us back!

The purpose of high-performance coaching is to help people find their motivation and overcome the barriers that hold them back. It is about the support you give them, as a coach, and about the challenge you create for them to explore their full potential.

You can use this type of coaching when:

- Long-range career or life planning – Some people prefer a chaotic life, without a life plan. But people with clear life goals are more likely to become successful in a long time than those without a concrete plan.

- Navigating career change points –
  The transition from the position of
  manager to leader for the team is
  clear evidence of change. Coaching
  helps people to manage this shift
  more successfully.

- Making fundamental changes to
  performance or behavior.

- Handling major life setbacks –
  Coaching will help people recover
  from business and personal
  setbacks: deal with stress or
  burnout.

High-performance Coaching skills and Tools

When you coach others you need to:

- Be respectful of the coachee

- Be respectful of the coachee's skills and goals in life

- Be honest in giving constructive and challenging feedback, and set high goals that the coachee is likely to accomplish.

- Be aware of your own ego, because it can get into the coachee's way.

- Try to use a large variety of coaching tools: The GROW Model, the FLOW Model and also the simple formula taken from one of the most valuable coaching books:

PERFORMANCE = POTENTIAL - INTERFERENCE

The FLOW Model

The balance between challenge and skills

If you have ever been so involved in a project or activity that you lost the track of time and your attention was focused entirely on what you were doing and you felt so engaged, energized, delighted, well this is called to be in flow. When it occurs, we lose the sense of self and become very devoted to the task that we move forward on instinct, without being conscious of our level of involvement.

The FLOW Model was first studied by the psychologist Mihaly Csikszentmihalyi in his book, *Flow – The Psychology of Optimal Experience.*

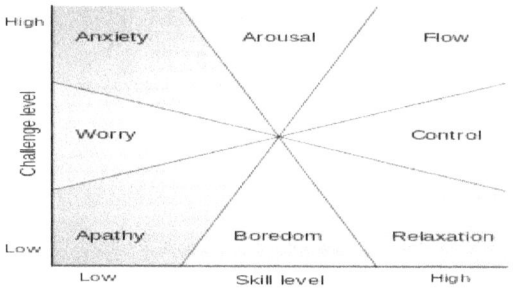

This model highlights the palette of

emotional states that we experience when we try to complete a task, depending on the level of difficulty of the challenge and our perceptions of our skill levels.

If the task is not challenging and you don't have to put a lot of effort in it, we are likely to feel apathy towards it.

When you face a challenging task without the required skills, you will feel anxious and worried about it.

In order to meet our challenges, you need well-developed skills, to conquer productivity techniques and be confident in your strengths.

To be in flow means to be absolutely engaged in your activity. You see a lot of people succeeding in life. They seem to have a perfect life, without worries and stress and it seems to be very easy, but the secret that they are really involved in what they do and they love what they do.

10 Components of FLOW

There are 10 components of the state of being in flow:

- Having a clear understanding of what you want to achieve

- Being able to focus on a sustained

period of time.

- Losing the feeling of being conscious of one's self.

- Finding that time passes quickly.

- Getting direct and quick feedback.

- Finding the balance between ability levels and challenge.

- Having a clear sense of personal control over the situation.

- Feeling that the activity is inner rewarding.

- Lacking consciousness of bodily needs.

- Being absolutely concentrated in

the activity itself.

There are Three Conditions of entering into the state of flow:

- Goals – Learning to set SMART Goals is one of the conditions of experiencing flow because they will help you achieve the focus you need.

- Balance – It is about the balance between the perceived skills and challenge of the task.

- Feedback – In order to improve your performance, the immediate feedback is very important. This will give you the sense of progress and you will become aware of the level of progress you achieved.

Using the FLOW Model

There are some tools that will improve your chances to experience the flow:

- Set Goals – Goal Setting adds motivation and structure.

- Improve the concentration – You need to use strategies to improve your concentration because it will make you more productive and focused.

- Build self-confidence – Without

confidence in your skills, every task will seem harder than it is.

- Get feedback – Give and receive feedback because this is the only way to help yourself and others to improve.

- Make your work more challenging – You should consider job crafting as an effective strategy to create job satisfaction.

- Improve your skills – Do a personal SWOT Analysis. It will help you determine the skills that you need to improve to be successful. You can then create your own plan in order to accomplish challenging tasks. A

Personal Development Plan Workbook shows you the process more detailed.

- Coach yourself – Learn how to coach yourself if you don't have a mentor or a coach...It will be very challenging and you will gain more confidence in your skills and strengths.

Emotional Interference

Gallwey's simple formula says that: Performance=Potential-Interference

Interference mean here emotional interference because our performance is clouded by the negative emotions we sometimes feel and get in our way, even if we have a clear understanding of our potential.

These interfering emotions are fear, guilt and worry.

- **Fear** – is the most inhibiting emotion. Maybe some are the product of our reality, but many of them are insubstantial. Our minds play negative games to keep us in a safe world, but also unchallenged and unfulfilled. The first step in solving the problem is to recognize your fears and to discuss them with people because you weaken their power to affect your performance. It is also beneficial to anticipate the worst-case scenarios. You will be more prepared to embrace failure and you won't be shocked by its negative impact.

- **Guilt** – this provides an improper work-life balance. If someone asks you to help him with a task, you will help him because you are not able to say no. This is based on a form of guilt,

- **Worry** – it can lead to physical problems such as poor quality sleep, bad eating habits and exhaustion. You can work effectively with these problems for a long time.

The duty of a coach is to help the coachee to find the true potential and erase the impact and effect of interfering emotions. You need to listen and understand what drives people and appreciate their emotions and then to help coachee explore the skills they need to their very best.

"The growth and development of people is the highest calling of coaching."

Chapter 25: Create a high-performance team

The reason why corporations cave in is not because the chairs are not of the best quality or because the floors are not glossy-tiled. They collapse because the people steering their wheels are not visionary enough. A visionary leader is not the one who relies on their own abilities because they cannot be in charge of every department. You must learn how to delegate tasks as a leader. And for delegation to work, one needs to have a highly motivated army of team members who are not only equipped with the right skills but also ones who have the right attitude.

As such, this piece explores a number of tips to nurture a team of highly motivated staff. Three cardinal aspects of creating a powerful team that is discussed below are: building strong relationships, nurturing accountability, and doing excellent networking. Read on.

1. How to Nurture Strong Relationship

Nurturing strong professional relationship is not easy as a leader. First, it is imperative to ensure that your subordinates do not view you as the big boss'. Instead, they should see you as a fellow team member who is only the captain of the crew. Instead of inspiring fear, you should engineer a sense of mutual respect, understand, and a strong feeling of camaraderie/fellowship. Know everyone and let them know themselves. Any organization should have a well-rounded distribution of skills and competences. Tap into everyone's strongest points and boost productivity as you cultivate a sense of cordial friendliness.

2. The Importance of Accountability

Any organization that does not have a clear chain of accountability is bound to fail. Although self-accountability has to be the principal motivation, everyone cannot be left to their own devices. As such, people have to know who are above them and who are below them. The overall goal of this arrangement is not to inspire fear but make people aware of how tasks should be executed. When followers know that that there is a strong chain of accountability, they will be kept on track since they know that any blunder will be soon unmasked and the necessary steps taken.

3. The Benefits of Networking

Many people know the importance external networking but may not be very familiar with internal networking. When networking is encouraged, people are able to enlist the insight of others when tackling particularly thorny professional or technical jigsaws. Since there is never a new problem, networking enables employees to tap into the experience of their counterparts which have faced similar hurdles before.

Conclusion

The idea of this book was to reflect the coaching process through leadership. Coaching can't be done without learning to be a leader for your team and your people. Once you have mastered the tools of leadership, you will find that coaching is the most powerful form of leadership you can practice.

Leaders with the proper coaching skills can motivate direct reports and work with bosses and peers in a manner that reduces dissensions and enhances productivity.

Today, more and more organizations are using coaching to increase performance and expand talent at each level. It will motivate employees and increase engagement, build the capacity for self-direction, facilitate team performance, address performance issues, improve peer relationships and practices.Why do you need leadership coaching today?In this changing global economy, the ability to implement change and strengthen performance is an essential leadership coaching skill.

1. Create your vision – Leading change

It increases the awareness of your leadership coaching strengths as well as gets in the way of using those strengths in difficult situations. It solidifies your skills in your default leadership style. It shapes the components of a strong vision and develops a real world vision for change in your organization. You will be able to implement that change through a specific strategy.

- Develop a strong comprehension of your default leadership style
- Explore where that style helps and hinders your leadership coaching performance

- Explore the components of a powerful vision
- Develop a vision for change

2. Remove the roadblocks – a new take on corporate change strategy

It means delving deeper into your change vision. This focuses on the systematic and people challenges of change and offers a simple but effective method for implementing change from inception to pre-implementation.

- Sharpen your change vision into an effective change initiative

- Identify roadblocks to implementing your change initiative
- Obtain tools to remove roadblocks to change
- Gain the awareness and tools to highlight corporate culture
- Empower change to drive real performance improvements

3. Lead others

   You will identify how to give people what they need to create stronger relationships, increased effectiveness, and a high-performance workplace. People engage in change only because they want to do this, that's why you have to discover how to motivate them because everyone is unique. You have to determine them to be responsible for their decisions or tasks and hold them accountable.

- Achieve leadership mentoring skills
- Motivate people through a set of values
- Cultivate the art of influencing
- Inspire people
- Remove the barriers between people

I hope you understood through this amount of information the importance of leadership coaching for achieving performance in an organization or team.

Thank you for purchasing and reading my book. I hope you have enjoyed it and you have received the value that I have put in it.

www.ingramcontent.com/pod-product-compliance
Lightning Source LLC
Chambersburg PA
CBHW051859170526
45168CB00001B/169